50 Flavor-Packed Roasted Veggies

By: Kelly Johnson

Table of Contents

- Roasted Sweet Potatoes with Cinnamon and Honey
- Balsamic Roasted Brussels Sprouts
- Herb-Roasted Carrots with Garlic
- Roasted Cauliflower with Lemon and Tahini
- Spicy Roasted Cauliflower with Curry
- Lemon and Dill Roasted Zucchini
- Roasted Bell Peppers with Feta and Olives
- Garlic-Parmesan Roasted Asparagus
- Roasted Butternut Squash with Sage
- Smoked Paprika Roasted Eggplant
- Roasted Beetroot with Thyme and Garlic
- Roasted Broccoli with Lemon Zest
- Maple-Roasted Parsnips
- Caramelized Red Onions with Balsamic Vinegar
- Spicy Roasted Brussels Sprouts with Sriracha
- Roasted Mushrooms with Thyme and Balsamic
- Roasted Sweet Potatoes with Black Beans
- Garlic and Herb Roasted Tomatoes
- Roasted Fennel with Orange and Olive Oil
- Spicy Roasted Acorn Squash
- Roasted Baby Carrots with Honey and Dill
- Roasted Cabbage with Mustard and Apple Cider Vinegar
- Lemon and Rosemary Roasted Potatoes
- Roasted Root Vegetable Medley
- Cinnamon-Spiced Roasted Carrots
- Roasted Kale Chips with Sea Salt
- Roasted Radishes with Olive Oil and Garlic
- Roasted Brussel Sprouts with Bacon and Parmesan
- Roasted Garlic and Herb Fingerling Potatoes
- Roasted Artichokes with Lemon and Olive Oil
- Roasted Zucchini and Eggplant with Basil
- Mediterranean Roasted Vegetables with Oregano
- Honey Roasted Parsnips and Carrots
- Roasted Beets with Goat Cheese and Walnuts
- Roasted Sweet Potatoes with Chipotle

- Roasted Summer Squash with Garlic and Parsley
- Garlic Butter Roasted Corn on the Cob
- Roasted Rutabaga with Caraway Seeds
- Roasted Pumpkin with Cinnamon and Nutmeg
- Lemon and Basil Roasted Tomatoes
- Roasted Broccoli and Cauliflower with Parmesan
- Roasted Red Bell Peppers with Garlic and Basil
- Roasted Brussel Sprouts with Lemon and Almonds
- Roasted Mushrooms with Balsamic Vinegar
- Roasted Peppers with Garlic and Oregano
- Roasted Winter Squash with Maple Syrup
- Smoky Roasted Eggplant with Cumin
- Spicy Roasted Sweet Potato and Black Bean Salad
- Roasted Jalapeño and Corn Salsa
- Roasted Vegetable Tacos with Lime Crema

Roasted Sweet Potatoes with Cinnamon and Honey

Ingredients:

- 3 medium sweet potatoes, peeled and cubed
- 2 tbsp olive oil
- 1 tsp ground cinnamon
- 2 tbsp honey
- Salt, to taste

Instructions:

1. **Preheat oven** – Set to 400°F (200°C).
2. **Prepare potatoes** – Toss cubed sweet potatoes with olive oil, cinnamon, and salt.
3. **Roast** – Spread on a baking sheet and roast for 25–30 minutes, flipping halfway through.
4. **Finish** – Drizzle with honey and serve warm.

Balsamic Roasted Brussels Sprouts

Ingredients:

- 1 lb Brussels sprouts, trimmed and halved
- 2 tbsp olive oil
- 2 tbsp balsamic vinegar
- Salt and pepper, to taste

Instructions:

1. **Preheat oven** – Set to 375°F (190°C).
2. **Prepare Brussels sprouts** – Toss Brussels sprouts with olive oil, balsamic vinegar, salt, and pepper.
3. **Roast** – Spread on a baking sheet and roast for 20–25 minutes, shaking the pan halfway through.
4. **Serve** – Enjoy warm.

Herb-Roasted Carrots with Garlic

Ingredients:

- 6 large carrots, peeled and cut into sticks
- 2 tbsp olive oil
- 3 garlic cloves, minced
- 1 tbsp fresh thyme, chopped
- Salt and pepper, to taste

Instructions:

1. **Preheat oven** – Set to 400°F (200°C).
2. **Prepare carrots** – Toss carrots with olive oil, garlic, thyme, salt, and pepper.
3. **Roast** – Spread on a baking sheet and roast for 25–30 minutes, stirring halfway through.
4. **Serve** – Garnish with additional fresh thyme if desired.

Roasted Cauliflower with Lemon and Tahini

Ingredients:

- 1 head of cauliflower, cut into florets
- 2 tbsp olive oil
- 2 tbsp tahini
- 1 tbsp lemon juice
- 1 tsp lemon zest
- Salt and pepper, to taste

Instructions:

1. **Preheat oven** – Set to 400°F (200°C).
2. **Prepare cauliflower** – Toss cauliflower florets with olive oil, salt, and pepper.
3. **Roast** – Spread on a baking sheet and roast for 25–30 minutes.
4. **Finish** – In a small bowl, mix tahini, lemon juice, and zest. Drizzle over roasted cauliflower and serve.

Spicy Roasted Cauliflower with Curry

Ingredients:

- 1 head of cauliflower, cut into florets
- 2 tbsp olive oil
- 1 tbsp curry powder
- ½ tsp cayenne pepper
- Salt, to taste

Instructions:

1. **Preheat oven** – Set to 400°F (200°C).
2. **Prepare cauliflower** – Toss cauliflower with olive oil, curry powder, cayenne, and salt.
3. **Roast** – Spread on a baking sheet and roast for 25–30 minutes, until golden and tender.
4. **Serve** – Enjoy warm as a side dish.

Lemon and Dill Roasted Zucchini

Ingredients:

- 4 medium zucchinis, sliced into rounds
- 2 tbsp olive oil
- 1 tbsp fresh dill, chopped
- Zest and juice of 1 lemon
- Salt and pepper, to taste

Instructions:

1. **Preheat oven** – Set to 400°F (200°C).
2. **Prepare zucchini** – Toss zucchini slices with olive oil, dill, lemon zest, lemon juice, salt, and pepper.
3. **Roast** – Spread on a baking sheet and roast for 15–20 minutes, flipping halfway through.
4. **Serve** – Serve warm as a side dish.

Roasted Bell Peppers with Feta and Olives

Ingredients:

- 4 bell peppers, cut into halves and seeded
- 2 tbsp olive oil
- ½ cup feta cheese, crumbled
- ¼ cup Kalamata olives, pitted and chopped
- 1 tbsp fresh oregano, chopped
- Salt and pepper, to taste

Instructions:

1. **Preheat oven** – Set to 375°F (190°C).
2. **Prepare peppers** – Toss pepper halves with olive oil, salt, and pepper.
3. **Roast** – Place peppers cut side down on a baking sheet and roast for 20–25 minutes.
4. **Finish** – Remove from oven and sprinkle with feta, olives, and oregano before serving.

Garlic-Parmesan Roasted Asparagus

Ingredients:

- 1 bunch asparagus, trimmed
- 2 tbsp olive oil
- 2 garlic cloves, minced
- ½ cup grated Parmesan cheese
- Salt and pepper, to taste

Instructions:

1. **Preheat oven** – Set to 400°F (200°C).
2. **Prepare asparagus** – Toss asparagus with olive oil, garlic, salt, and pepper.
3. **Roast** – Spread asparagus on a baking sheet and roast for 15–20 minutes, until tender.
4. **Finish** – Sprinkle with Parmesan cheese and serve warm.

Roasted Butternut Squash with Sage

Ingredients:

- 1 small butternut squash, peeled and cubed
- 2 tbsp olive oil
- 1 tbsp fresh sage, chopped
- Salt and pepper, to taste

Instructions:

1. **Preheat oven** – Set to 400°F (200°C).
2. **Prepare squash** – Toss squash cubes with olive oil, sage, salt, and pepper.
3. **Roast** – Spread on a baking sheet and roast for 25–30 minutes, flipping halfway through.
4. **Serve** – Garnish with additional fresh sage if desired.

Smoked Paprika Roasted Eggplant

Ingredients:

- 2 medium eggplants, sliced into rounds
- 2 tbsp olive oil
- 1 tsp smoked paprika
- Salt and pepper, to taste

Instructions:

1. **Preheat oven** – Set to 400°F (200°C).
2. **Prepare eggplant** – Toss eggplant slices with olive oil, smoked paprika, salt, and pepper.
3. **Roast** – Spread on a baking sheet and roast for 20–25 minutes, until golden and tender.
4. **Serve** – Serve warm as a side dish or appetizer.

Roasted Beetroot with Thyme and Garlic

Ingredients:

- 4 medium beets, peeled and cut into wedges
- 2 tbsp olive oil
- 3 garlic cloves, minced
- 1 tbsp fresh thyme, chopped
- Salt and pepper, to taste

Instructions:

1. **Preheat oven** – Set to 375°F (190°C).
2. **Prepare beets** – Toss beet wedges with olive oil, garlic, thyme, salt, and pepper.
3. **Roast** – Spread on a baking sheet and roast for 30–40 minutes, flipping halfway through.
4. **Serve** – Garnish with additional fresh thyme if desired.

Roasted Broccoli with Lemon Zest

Ingredients:

- 1 head of broccoli, cut into florets
- 2 tbsp olive oil
- Zest of 1 lemon
- Salt and pepper, to taste

Instructions:

1. **Preheat oven** – Set to 400°F (200°C).
2. **Prepare broccoli** – Toss broccoli florets with olive oil, lemon zest, salt, and pepper.
3. **Roast** – Spread on a baking sheet and roast for 20–25 minutes, shaking the pan halfway through.
4. **Serve** – Enjoy warm.

Maple-Roasted Parsnips

Ingredients:

- 4 medium parsnips, peeled and cut into sticks
- 2 tbsp olive oil
- 2 tbsp maple syrup
- Salt and pepper, to taste

Instructions:

1. **Preheat oven** – Set to 400°F (200°C).
2. **Prepare parsnips** – Toss parsnips with olive oil, maple syrup, salt, and pepper.
3. **Roast** – Spread on a baking sheet and roast for 25–30 minutes, flipping halfway through.
4. **Serve** – Enjoy the sweet, caramelized flavors.

Caramelized Red Onions with Balsamic Vinegar

Ingredients:

- 2 large red onions, thinly sliced
- 2 tbsp olive oil
- 2 tbsp balsamic vinegar
- 1 tsp sugar
- Salt and pepper, to taste

Instructions:

1. **Preheat oven** – Set to 375°F (190°C).
2. **Prepare onions** – Toss onions with olive oil, balsamic vinegar, sugar, salt, and pepper.
3. **Roast** – Spread on a baking sheet and roast for 30–35 minutes, stirring halfway through.
4. **Serve** – Serve as a topping for roasted vegetables or meats.

Spicy Roasted Brussels Sprouts with Sriracha

Ingredients:

- 1 lb Brussels sprouts, trimmed and halved
- 2 tbsp olive oil
- 1 tbsp Sriracha sauce
- 1 tbsp honey
- Salt and pepper, to taste

Instructions:

1. **Preheat oven** – Set to 400°F (200°C).
2. **Prepare Brussels sprouts** – Toss Brussels sprouts with olive oil, Sriracha, honey, salt, and pepper.
3. **Roast** – Spread on a baking sheet and roast for 20–25 minutes, flipping halfway through.
4. **Serve** – Serve warm, with extra Sriracha for heat if desired.

Roasted Mushrooms with Thyme and Balsamic

Ingredients:

- 16 oz button mushrooms, halved
- 2 tbsp olive oil
- 1 tbsp fresh thyme, chopped
- 2 tbsp balsamic vinegar
- Salt and pepper, to taste

Instructions:

1. **Preheat oven** – Set to 400°F (200°C).
2. **Prepare mushrooms** – Toss mushrooms with olive oil, thyme, balsamic vinegar, salt, and pepper.
3. **Roast** – Spread on a baking sheet and roast for 20–25 minutes.
4. **Serve** – Garnish with additional fresh thyme if desired.

Roasted Sweet Potatoes with Black Beans

Ingredients:

- 2 large sweet potatoes, peeled and cubed
- 1 tbsp olive oil
- 1 tsp cumin
- 1 tsp paprika
- 1 can black beans, drained and rinsed
- Salt and pepper, to taste

Instructions:

1. **Preheat oven** – Set to 400°F (200°C).
2. **Prepare sweet potatoes** – Toss sweet potato cubes with olive oil, cumin, paprika, salt, and pepper.
3. **Roast** – Spread on a baking sheet and roast for 25–30 minutes, flipping halfway through.
4. **Finish** – Toss roasted sweet potatoes with black beans and serve warm.

Garlic and Herb Roasted Tomatoes

Ingredients:

- 2 cups cherry tomatoes, halved
- 2 tbsp olive oil
- 2 garlic cloves, minced
- 1 tbsp fresh basil, chopped
- Salt and pepper, to taste

Instructions:

1. **Preheat oven** – Set to 375°F (190°C).
2. **Prepare tomatoes** – Toss tomatoes with olive oil, garlic, basil, salt, and pepper.
3. **Roast** – Spread on a baking sheet and roast for 15–20 minutes.
4. **Serve** – Serve as a side dish or topping for salads and pastas.

Roasted Fennel with Orange and Olive Oil

Ingredients:

- 2 fennel bulbs, sliced
- 2 tbsp olive oil
- Zest and juice of 1 orange
- Salt and pepper, to taste

Instructions:

1. **Preheat oven** – Set to 400°F (200°C).
2. **Prepare fennel** – Toss fennel slices with olive oil, orange zest, orange juice, salt, and pepper.
3. **Roast** – Spread on a baking sheet and roast for 25–30 minutes, until golden and tender.
4. **Serve** – Enjoy the citrusy flavor of the fennel.

Spicy Roasted Acorn Squash

Ingredients:

- 2 acorn squash, halved and seeds removed
- 2 tbsp olive oil
- 1 tsp ground cumin
- ½ tsp chili powder
- ¼ tsp cayenne pepper
- Salt and pepper, to taste

Instructions:

1. **Preheat oven** – Set to 400°F (200°C).
2. **Prepare squash** – Drizzle acorn squash halves with olive oil, then sprinkle with cumin, chili powder, cayenne, salt, and pepper.
3. **Roast** – Place squash halves cut-side down on a baking sheet and roast for 30–35 minutes, until tender.
4. **Serve** – Serve warm as a flavorful side dish.

Roasted Baby Carrots with Honey and Dill

Ingredients:

- 1 lb baby carrots, peeled
- 2 tbsp olive oil
- 1 tbsp honey
- 1 tbsp fresh dill, chopped
- Salt and pepper, to taste

Instructions:

1. **Preheat oven** – Set to 400°F (200°C).
2. **Prepare carrots** – Toss baby carrots with olive oil, honey, dill, salt, and pepper.
3. **Roast** – Spread carrots on a baking sheet and roast for 20–25 minutes, until tender and caramelized.
4. **Serve** – Serve warm with an extra sprinkle of fresh dill.

Roasted Cabbage with Mustard and Apple Cider Vinegar

Ingredients:

- 1 small head of cabbage, sliced into wedges
- 2 tbsp olive oil
- 1 tbsp Dijon mustard
- 1 tbsp apple cider vinegar
- Salt and pepper, to taste

Instructions:

1. **Preheat oven** – Set to 400°F (200°C).
2. **Prepare cabbage** – Toss cabbage wedges with olive oil, mustard, apple cider vinegar, salt, and pepper.
3. **Roast** – Spread cabbage wedges on a baking sheet and roast for 20–25 minutes, flipping halfway through.
4. **Serve** – Serve as a tangy, roasted side dish.

Lemon and Rosemary Roasted Potatoes

Ingredients:

- 1 ½ lbs small baby potatoes, halved
- 2 tbsp olive oil
- 1 tbsp fresh rosemary, chopped
- Zest and juice of 1 lemon
- Salt and pepper, to taste

Instructions:

1. **Preheat oven** – Set to 400°F (200°C).
2. **Prepare potatoes** – Toss halved potatoes with olive oil, rosemary, lemon zest, lemon juice, salt, and pepper.
3. **Roast** – Spread potatoes on a baking sheet and roast for 25–30 minutes, flipping halfway through.
4. **Serve** – Serve warm, garnished with additional rosemary if desired.

Roasted Root Vegetable Medley

Ingredients:

- 1 medium sweet potato, peeled and cubed
- 2 carrots, peeled and cut into sticks
- 1 parsnip, peeled and sliced
- 1 tbsp olive oil
- 1 tsp dried thyme
- Salt and pepper, to taste

Instructions:

1. **Preheat oven** – Set to 400°F (200°C).
2. **Prepare vegetables** – Toss sweet potatoes, carrots, and parsnips with olive oil, thyme, salt, and pepper.
3. **Roast** – Spread vegetables on a baking sheet and roast for 25–30 minutes, flipping halfway through.
4. **Serve** – Serve the medley warm as a hearty side dish.

Cinnamon-Spiced Roasted Carrots

Ingredients:

- 6 large carrots, peeled and cut into sticks
- 2 tbsp olive oil
- 1 tsp ground cinnamon
- 1 tbsp honey
- Salt, to taste

Instructions:

1. **Preheat oven** – Set to 375°F (190°C).
2. **Prepare carrots** – Toss carrots with olive oil, cinnamon, honey, and salt.
3. **Roast** – Spread carrots on a baking sheet and roast for 25–30 minutes, until tender.
4. **Serve** – Serve warm for a sweet and spiced side dish.

Roasted Kale Chips with Sea Salt

Ingredients:

- 1 bunch kale, stems removed and leaves torn
- 2 tbsp olive oil
- ½ tsp sea salt

Instructions:

1. **Preheat oven** – Set to 350°F (175°C).
2. **Prepare kale** – Toss kale leaves with olive oil and sea salt.
3. **Roast** – Spread kale on a baking sheet in a single layer and bake for 10–15 minutes, until crispy.
4. **Serve** – Serve immediately for a healthy and crunchy snack.

Roasted Radishes with Olive Oil and Garlic

Ingredients:

- 1 lb radishes, halved
- 2 tbsp olive oil
- 3 garlic cloves, minced
- Salt and pepper, to taste

Instructions:

1. **Preheat oven** – Set to 400°F (200°C).
2. **Prepare radishes** – Toss radishes with olive oil, garlic, salt, and pepper.
3. **Roast** – Spread radishes on a baking sheet and roast for 20–25 minutes, flipping halfway through.
4. **Serve** – Serve warm as a flavorful side dish.

Roasted Brussel Sprouts with Bacon and Parmesan

Ingredients:

- 1 lb Brussels sprouts, trimmed and halved
- 2 tbsp olive oil
- 4 slices bacon, chopped
- ¼ cup grated Parmesan cheese
- Salt and pepper, to taste

Instructions:

1. **Preheat oven** – Set to 400°F (200°C).
2. **Prepare Brussels sprouts** – Toss Brussels sprouts with olive oil, salt, and pepper.
3. **Roast** – Spread Brussels sprouts on a baking sheet and roast for 20 minutes.
4. **Cook bacon** – While sprouts roast, cook bacon in a skillet until crispy, then drain.
5. **Finish** – Sprinkle roasted Brussels sprouts with bacon and Parmesan before serving.

Roasted Garlic and Herb Fingerling Potatoes

Ingredients:

- 1 lb fingerling potatoes, halved
- 3 garlic cloves, minced
- 2 tbsp olive oil
- 1 tbsp fresh rosemary, chopped
- Salt and pepper, to taste

Instructions:

1. **Preheat oven** – Set to 400°F (200°C).
2. **Prepare potatoes** – Toss fingerling potatoes with garlic, olive oil, rosemary, salt, and pepper.
3. **Roast** – Spread potatoes on a baking sheet and roast for 25–30 minutes, flipping halfway through.
4. **Serve** – Serve warm as a delicious side dish.

Roasted Artichokes with Lemon and Olive Oil

Ingredients:

- 2 artichokes, trimmed and halved
- 3 tbsp olive oil
- Juice of 1 lemon
- Salt and pepper, to taste

Instructions:

1. **Preheat oven** – Set to 375°F (190°C).
2. **Prepare artichokes** – Drizzle artichoke halves with olive oil, lemon juice, salt, and pepper.
3. **Roast** – Place artichokes cut-side down on a baking sheet and roast for 40–45 minutes.
4. **Serve** – Serve warm with extra lemon wedges on the side.

Roasted Zucchini and Eggplant with Basil

Ingredients:

- 2 zucchinis, sliced
- 1 eggplant, sliced
- 2 tbsp olive oil
- 1 tbsp fresh basil, chopped
- Salt and pepper, to taste

Instructions:

1. **Preheat oven** – Set to 400°F (200°C).
2. **Prepare vegetables** – Toss zucchini and eggplant slices with olive oil, basil, salt, and pepper.
3. **Roast** – Spread vegetables on a baking sheet and roast for 20–25 minutes, until tender.
4. **Serve** – Garnish with additional basil and serve warm.

Mediterranean Roasted Vegetables with Oregano

Ingredients:

- 1 red bell pepper, chopped
- 1 yellow bell pepper, chopped
- 1 zucchini, chopped
- 1 red onion, chopped
- 2 tbsp olive oil
- 1 tbsp dried oregano
- Salt and pepper, to taste

Instructions:

1. **Preheat oven** – Set to 375°F (190°C).
2. **Prepare vegetables** – Toss bell peppers, zucchini, and onion with olive oil, oregano, salt, and pepper.
3. **Roast** – Spread vegetables on a baking sheet and roast for 25–30 minutes, stirring halfway through.
4. **Serve** – Serve warm as a flavorful Mediterranean side.

Honey Roasted Parsnips and Carrots

Ingredients:

- 3 large parsnips, peeled and sliced
- 4 medium carrots, peeled and sliced
- 2 tbsp olive oil
- 2 tbsp honey
- Salt and pepper, to taste

Instructions:

1. **Preheat oven** – Set to 400°F (200°C).
2. **Prepare vegetables** – Toss parsnips and carrots with olive oil, honey, salt, and pepper.
3. **Roast** – Spread on a baking sheet and roast for 25–30 minutes, flipping halfway through.
4. **Serve** – Serve warm with a drizzle of honey if desired.

Roasted Beets with Goat Cheese and Walnuts

Ingredients:

- 4 medium beets, peeled and cubed
- 2 tbsp olive oil
- 1 tbsp balsamic vinegar
- ¼ cup crumbled goat cheese
- ¼ cup toasted walnuts
- Salt and pepper, to taste

Instructions:

1. **Preheat oven** – Set to 400°F (200°C).
2. **Prepare beets** – Toss beets with olive oil, balsamic vinegar, salt, and pepper.
3. **Roast** – Spread beets on a baking sheet and roast for 30–40 minutes, until tender.
4. **Finish** – Garnish with goat cheese and walnuts before serving.

Roasted Sweet Potatoes with Chipotle

Ingredients:

- 3 medium sweet potatoes, peeled and cubed
- 2 tbsp olive oil
- 1 tsp chipotle powder
- 1 tbsp maple syrup
- Salt, to taste

Instructions:

1. **Preheat oven** – Set to 400°F (200°C).
2. **Prepare sweet potatoes** – Toss sweet potato cubes with olive oil, chipotle powder, maple syrup, and salt.
3. **Roast** – Spread on a baking sheet and roast for 25–30 minutes, flipping halfway through.
4. **Serve** – Serve warm for a smoky-sweet side dish.

Roasted Summer Squash with Garlic and Parsley

Ingredients:

- 2 medium summer squash, sliced
- 3 garlic cloves, minced
- 2 tbsp olive oil
- 2 tbsp fresh parsley, chopped
- Salt and pepper, to taste

Instructions:

1. **Preheat oven** – Set to 375°F (190°C).
2. **Prepare squash** – Toss squash slices with garlic, olive oil, salt, and pepper.
3. **Roast** – Spread on a baking sheet and roast for 15–20 minutes, until tender.
4. **Serve** – Garnish with fresh parsley and serve warm.

Garlic Butter Roasted Corn on the Cob

Ingredients:

- 4 ears of corn, husked
- 4 tbsp unsalted butter, melted
- 3 garlic cloves, minced
- 1 tbsp fresh parsley, chopped
- Salt and pepper, to taste

Instructions:

1. **Preheat oven** – Set to 400°F (200°C).
2. **Prepare corn** – Brush corn with melted butter, garlic, salt, and pepper.
3. **Roast** – Place corn directly on the oven rack or on a baking sheet and roast for 20–25 minutes.
4. **Serve** – Sprinkle with fresh parsley and serve warm.

Roasted Rutabaga with Caraway Seeds

Ingredients:

- 2 medium rutabagas, peeled and cubed
- 2 tbsp olive oil
- 1 tsp caraway seeds
- Salt and pepper, to taste

Instructions:

1. **Preheat oven** – Set to 400°F (200°C).
2. **Prepare rutabaga** – Toss rutabaga cubes with olive oil, caraway seeds, salt, and pepper.
3. **Roast** – Spread on a baking sheet and roast for 30–35 minutes, flipping halfway through.
4. **Serve** – Serve warm as a savory root vegetable side.

Roasted Pumpkin with Cinnamon and Nutmeg

Ingredients:

- 1 medium pumpkin, peeled, seeded, and cubed
- 2 tbsp olive oil
- 1 tsp ground cinnamon
- ½ tsp ground nutmeg
- Salt and pepper, to taste

Instructions:

1. **Preheat oven** – Set to 375°F (190°C).
2. **Prepare pumpkin** – Toss pumpkin cubes with olive oil, cinnamon, nutmeg, salt, and pepper.
3. **Roast** – Spread pumpkin on a baking sheet and roast for 25–30 minutes, until tender.
4. **Serve** – Serve warm as a sweet and aromatic side dish.

Lemon and Basil Roasted Tomatoes

Ingredients:

- 2 cups cherry tomatoes, halved
- 2 tbsp olive oil
- Zest and juice of 1 lemon
- 1 tbsp fresh basil, chopped
- Salt and pepper, to taste

Instructions:

1. **Preheat oven** – Set to 400°F (200°C).
2. **Prepare tomatoes** – Toss tomatoes with olive oil, lemon zest, lemon juice, basil, salt, and pepper.
3. **Roast** – Spread tomatoes on a baking sheet and roast for 15–20 minutes, until soft and caramelized.
4. **Serve** – Serve warm as a fresh, zesty side dish.

Roasted Broccoli and Cauliflower with Parmesan

Ingredients:

- 1 cup broccoli florets
- 1 cup cauliflower florets
- 2 tbsp olive oil
- ½ cup grated Parmesan cheese
- 1 tsp garlic powder
- Salt and pepper, to taste

Instructions:

1. **Preheat oven** – Set to 400°F (200°C).
2. **Prepare vegetables** – Toss broccoli and cauliflower with olive oil, garlic powder, salt, and pepper.
3. **Roast** – Spread on a baking sheet and roast for 20–25 minutes, until tender and slightly crispy.
4. **Finish** – Sprinkle with grated Parmesan cheese and serve warm.

Roasted Red Bell Peppers with Garlic and Basil

Ingredients:

- 4 red bell peppers, halved and seeded
- 3 garlic cloves, minced
- 2 tbsp olive oil
- 1 tbsp fresh basil, chopped
- Salt and pepper, to taste

Instructions:

1. **Preheat oven** – Set to 375°F (190°C).
2. **Prepare peppers** – Place bell pepper halves on a baking sheet, skin side up. Drizzle with olive oil, minced garlic, salt, and pepper.
3. **Roast** – Roast for 20–25 minutes, until the skin is charred and tender.
4. **Finish** – Remove skins, sprinkle with fresh basil, and serve warm.

Roasted Brussel Sprouts with Lemon and Almonds

Ingredients:

- 1 lb Brussels sprouts, trimmed and halved
- 2 tbsp olive oil
- 1 tbsp lemon juice
- ¼ cup sliced almonds
- Salt and pepper, to taste

Instructions:

1. **Preheat oven** – Set to 400°F (200°C).
2. **Prepare Brussels sprouts** – Toss Brussels sprouts with olive oil, lemon juice, salt, and pepper.
3. **Roast** – Spread Brussels sprouts on a baking sheet and roast for 20–25 minutes, flipping halfway through.
4. **Finish** – Sprinkle with sliced almonds and serve warm.

Roasted Mushrooms with Balsamic Vinegar

Ingredients:

- 16 oz mushrooms, halved
- 2 tbsp olive oil
- 1 tbsp balsamic vinegar
- 1 tsp fresh thyme, chopped
- Salt and pepper, to taste

Instructions:

1. **Preheat oven** – Set to 375°F (190°C).
2. **Prepare mushrooms** – Toss mushrooms with olive oil, balsamic vinegar, thyme, salt, and pepper.
3. **Roast** – Spread on a baking sheet and roast for 20–25 minutes, until tender and golden.
4. **Serve** – Serve warm as a flavorful side or topping for dishes.

Roasted Peppers with Garlic and Oregano

Ingredients:

- 4 red bell peppers, cut into strips
- 3 garlic cloves, minced
- 2 tbsp olive oil
- 1 tbsp dried oregano
- Salt and pepper, to taste

Instructions:

1. **Preheat oven** – Set to 400°F (200°C).
2. **Prepare peppers** – Toss pepper strips with olive oil, garlic, oregano, salt, and pepper.
3. **Roast** – Spread peppers on a baking sheet and roast for 20–25 minutes, until tender and slightly charred.
4. **Serve** – Serve warm as a savory side dish or topping for sandwiches and salads.

Roasted Winter Squash with Maple Syrup

Ingredients:

- 1 medium winter squash (such as butternut or acorn), peeled and cubed
- 2 tbsp olive oil
- 2 tbsp maple syrup
- Salt and pepper, to taste

Instructions:

1. **Preheat oven** – Set to 375°F (190°C).
2. **Prepare squash** – Toss squash cubes with olive oil, maple syrup, salt, and pepper.
3. **Roast** – Spread squash on a baking sheet and roast for 30–35 minutes, until golden and tender.
4. **Serve** – Serve warm as a sweet and savory side dish.

Smoky Roasted Eggplant with Cumin

Ingredients:

- 2 medium eggplants, cut into 1-inch cubes
- 2 tbsp olive oil
- 1 tsp ground cumin
- ½ tsp smoked paprika
- Salt and pepper, to taste

Instructions:

1. **Preheat oven** – Set to 400°F (200°C).
2. **Prepare eggplant** – Toss eggplant cubes with olive oil, cumin, smoked paprika, salt, and pepper.
3. **Roast** – Spread on a baking sheet and roast for 25–30 minutes, flipping halfway through.
4. **Serve** – Serve warm as a smoky, tender side dish or topping for grains.

Spicy Roasted Sweet Potato and Black Bean Salad

Ingredients:

- 2 medium sweet potatoes, peeled and cubed
- 1 tbsp olive oil
- 1 tsp chili powder
- 1 can black beans, drained and rinsed
- 1 avocado, diced
- 1 lime, juiced
- Salt and pepper, to taste

Instructions:

1. **Preheat oven** – Set to 400°F (200°C).
2. **Prepare sweet potatoes** – Toss sweet potato cubes with olive oil, chili powder, salt, and pepper.
3. **Roast** – Spread on a baking sheet and roast for 25–30 minutes, flipping halfway through.
4. **Assemble salad** – In a large bowl, combine roasted sweet potatoes, black beans, avocado, and lime juice.
5. **Serve** – Toss gently and serve warm or chilled.

Roasted Jalapeño and Corn Salsa

Ingredients:

- 4 fresh jalapeños, halved and seeded
- 2 cups corn kernels (fresh, frozen, or canned)
- 1 tbsp olive oil
- ½ red onion, chopped
- 1 tbsp fresh cilantro, chopped
- Juice of 1 lime
- Salt, to taste

Instructions:

1. **Preheat oven** – Set to 400°F (200°C).
2. **Prepare ingredients** – Toss jalapeños and corn with olive oil and place on a baking sheet.
3. **Roast** – Roast for 15–20 minutes, until the jalapeños are charred and the corn is golden.
4. **Assemble salsa** – Remove stems from roasted jalapeños and chop them. In a bowl, combine roasted jalapeños, corn, red onion, cilantro, lime juice, and salt.
5. **Serve** – Serve warm or chilled with chips, tacos, or grilled meats.

Roasted Vegetable Tacos with Lime Crema

Ingredients:

- 1 zucchini, sliced
- 1 bell pepper, chopped
- 1 red onion, chopped
- 1 tbsp olive oil
- 1 tsp chili powder
- ½ tsp cumin
- Salt and pepper, to taste
- 4 small corn tortillas
- 1/2 cup sour cream or Greek yogurt
- Juice of 1 lime
- Fresh cilantro, for garnish

Instructions:

1. **Preheat oven** – Set to 400°F (200°C).
2. **Prepare vegetables** – Toss zucchini, bell pepper, and red onion with olive oil, chili powder, cumin, salt, and pepper.
3. **Roast** – Spread vegetables on a baking sheet and roast for 20–25 minutes, until tender.
4. **Prepare crema** – In a small bowl, mix sour cream (or yogurt) with lime juice.
5. **Assemble tacos** – Warm tortillas and fill with roasted vegetables. Top with lime crema and fresh cilantro.
6. **Serve** – Serve warm as a flavorful vegetarian taco option.